BESOS

Original Poetry by: Celeste Alyssa Gomez

Editor: Efren Castro
Literary Assistant: Cassidi Mignuolo

Special thanks:

Feedback Proofreaders:
Efren Castro, Evan Ismail, & Rebecca Rodriguez

Feedback Contributors:
Melissa Tobias, Cian Ramirez, Gwen Benitez, Richard Gonzales, Patrice Gomez, Venezia Ramirez, Mikko Marimon, Lilana Tainatongo, Nayeli Vazquez-Montero, & Ashley Carbajal

Cover Art by: Shivangi Das

Author Photo: photographed by Reinhardt Kenneth & Rielle Oase

ACKNOWLEDGEMENTS

Special thanks to the Creative Writing department at the University of California, Riverside. I graduated in 2020, and every professor and human there is amazing. I remember entering college, not knowing what to expect as many of us feel when starting a new journey. The guidance and compassion I received from this department is something I will never forget and hold onto dearly as an artist. Besos, before it received a name, has been in the works since late 2018, and early 2019. Thank you to my professors; Sara Borjas, Michael Jayme, Kate Anger, Allison White, and Joshua Hardina for believing in my writing and providing me resources to become a stronger writer. I want to take time to thank the members of The Verbal Coliseum, my gratitude goes to Devany Harden and Lauren Marquez for welcoming me to the space and inspiring me. More inspiration and thanks to Ruth Madrid and Chelsea Ramirez, two bold creatives that taught me a lot. Lastly, much love and gratitude to Efren Castro, they're the editor for this project. In 2020, I reached out to them to help me proofread and provide feedback. During in days of this pandemic where I gave up on the book, Efren kept me on check not only as a friend, but as my creative coach. Thank you.

WORDS FROM THE BESOS TEAM

"My name is Cassidi Mignuolo and I had the amazing opportunity of being a literary assistant for the stunning poetry collection, 'Besos (Kisses)'. I have recently graduated from the University of California, Riverside with a B.A. in Sociology and a minor in Economics. Although my career aspirations are far from the literary world, I wanted to expand my knowledge with this project and challenge myself to do something a bit different. I can confidently say that these goals have been achieved and then some. I want to thank Celeste for being an incredible light in this journey and inspiring me with her courage to be so vulnerable with her writing. This is a phenomenal collection of works and I look forward to seeing how the literary world embraces her in the future!" -**Cassidi**

"My name is Efren Castro and I'm the editor for 'Besos,' I am a poet, zine-maker, and MFA student currently studying creative writing at UC Riverside. Being able to have the privilege of working on this project was such an amazing learning experience for me. I've gotten to know Celeste so intimately through this experience and I want to thank her for being so vulnerable with me and her work. This collection from Celeste is raw and honest, I hope her words find a home within you."
-**Efren**

DEDICATION

*To my mama and all
the loved ones in my life.
Thank you for your support.*

TRIGGER WARNING: The material in the sections are heavy content. If at any point, you need to place the book down, please do so. When your mind is refreshed, come back to the book. Know that I am with you during these poems. Thank you for taking the time to read my poetry.

-Besos

CONTENTS

Dawn 06

Recollection 52

Emotional 93

World 132

Crown 186

DAWN

your trauma is valid
and
you will rise
the sensations throughout
your body
will receive healing
from the shattered
parts of your soul
our pain
the
trauma is unwanted
and has placed us
in unsafe environments
that challenge our strength
we use our power
and together we rise

together we rise // *Besos*-C.A. Gomez

my healing is an art form
vivid and human
cultivated by my own pace
my body gives birth to all these memories
still and sturdy as a canvas
the paintbrush is a bandage
painting every creak and patching it into something much
more beautiful than anything you've ever seen
my body is the album of work you see
the portfolio you reread

portfolio // *Besos*-C.A. Gomez

when we were young
we thought we were in love
you were the hope and dream
i thought i needed
from loss to love
the past felt nonexistent
you presented yourself
as a positive affirmation
so i dodged the signs
your eyes looking into mine
in the evening
your silence still as water
but dangerous and deep as a wave
concealed by the moon
the deceiving smile you gave me
i the fool
continued to dance with you
you slowly took the sun with you
my light
my energy
became yours to control

foolish lovers // *Besos*-C.A. Gomez

we carved our initials on the tree
your hand laid on top of mine
we traced the letters
with our fingertips, then

we immersed our bodies to the grass
holding hands
smiling silently
i rolled my body to yours
capturing all our laughs

our hearts beating

then   left
    it   he

suddenly   stopped

    for us

maybe we were too young
to understand
what love really was
to be *loved* by you
evoked something
in me

corazón // *Besos*-C.A. Gomez

i don't believe we were destined
to be high school sweethearts
but i became comfortable
in settling
because i wanted an easy route
when life could provide me
so much more
i was willing to give it all away for you
i had no idea what i was doing
i wanted structure
a routine to rely on
that's what we were
four years of wandering

four years // *Besos-*C.A. Gomez

my self-esteem hit rock bottom
tumbling farther down into a hole
of
what if no one else wants me
what if no one else loves me
so my body was yours
would you ever love me like i loved you
i did not want to be alone
i told the universe that i'll surrender
my body if it promises me to never
leave me alone again
so it happened
sex

fear of you leaving me // *Besos*-C.A. Gomez

he made my body shapeshift
into a butterfly
with his magic
a delicate creature
not being able to see my wings
for how truly beautiful they are
my new body flew in the direction he wanted
with a flicker of magic from his fingertips
his abuse was not his goal
but control was
to keep my power in his hands
and my wings where he can guard them
simply because he felt that he had the right to
and i was too far away to see the truth

far // *Besos*-C.A. Gomez

him

you simply never think for yourself
wow, you really are an idiot aren't you
i'm too tired to deal with you right now

i felt that you were right
i felt too insecure to speak up
and i needed to do everything in my power
to have you stay
because you were all that i had

texts // *Besos*-C.A. Gomez

i would be a liar
if i said that you
didn't rent up
such space in my mind
our relationship
was just a lease
nothing long-lasting
and that's how it was
meant to be
you may have entered
my mind
but i've built a maze
so that it will get harder
for you to reach
the core

maze // *Besos*-C.A. Gomez

the taste of you
tainted my tongue
lingered in my mouth
my tongue searched
for happiness
when you fed me
anger, resentment,
distrust, and abuse
you were the enemy
since day one
a taste so sour
but i searched
for the old version
you fed me
i held onto
the old version of you
and craved
that familiar taste

new taste // *Besos-*C.A. Gomez

usted decidió crear este mundo conmigo, pero decidió enterrarlo cuando me abandonó, me engañó y me quemó con sus palabras de que el fuego llegó a las puntas de mis dedos

entrar en mi mundo // *Besos* -C.A. Gomez

i wanted to be held in your arms
hearing the pulsation of your heart
you could suffocate me
and i'd remain silent

pulse // *Besos*-C.A. Gomez

tell me how good she was
so i can practice
maybe pretend i'm her
i look at myself in the mirror
and see *her* in my eyes
i'm a complete mess
the moment you leave
i think you go straight to *her*
the cheating never left my head
i think about it most of the time
this pulse between you and i
has created an earthquake
shattering all trust
this delusion of love forms
this addiction

commitment // *Besos*-C.A. Gomez

the first mornings are the worst
i lie in bed and you are not here
my hand pats the other side
pretending it were you
even through all the pain
i loved you

first mornings // *Besos* -C.A. Gomez

i wonder how you sleep at night
knowing that the first time we had sex
my vagina bled
staining my sheets as a reminder of the pain
of unwanted sex
you said you loved me
and i believed it
this blood marked what came out of me
from your strokes
my pussy turned into a drawbridge
opening at your command

drawbridge // *Besos*-C.A. Gomez

your mouth was searching
for something sweet and thick
inside me
delving through the vines
the tongue of your mouth
sucked the layers of honey
building a home in me
while breaking mine
that is when my honey
turned into blood

honey blood // *Besos*-C.A. Gomez

sumérgete en mis palabras, que tus lágrimas te lleven a la orilla, que esta sea una lección de reflexión

me dijo // *Besos* -C.A. Gomez

i hear all these beautiful words from others
but not hearing them from you
kills me the most
one insult from you
is like a peckle of dust
that covers my throat
you glare
and keep feeding at the idea
my neck twists as if there were no bones
the sensations leave my fingertips
and your insults crush me

your words // *Besos* -C.A. Gomez

him

you're such a loser
this is why you will never get anywhere in life
you're such a woman

you can't hurt me anymore

texts // *Besos*-C.A. Gomez

Besos-26

when did you stop trying
and
when did i start becoming your rival

rival // *Besos*-C.A. Gomez

everyday with you
felt closer
to ending my life
your presence was like dawn
i could feel you coming
you thought
you were dawn
and that you could compose of
my body to the ground
your plan was to bury me
in the same grounds
as my mama
that is where i saw myself
dead

dawn // *Besos* -C.A. Gomez

mi amor
mi vida
mi muerte
mi cielo
mi angustia
mi sueño
mi lucha
mi comodidad
mi ciclo continuo

mi... // *Besos*-C.A. Gomez

i learned how to lose my heart quickly
by saying i love you too much
i wonder if i kept those words to myself
how things would have played out
after all the damage
i didn't feel strong enough to piece
everything around me together
i just wanted to feel needed
i'm sorry if i couldn't keep up with my emotions
i'm sorry if i loved too hard
i'm sorry that i wanted to feel needed
i wished you respected me more
instead of being greedy with it
your respect was there when you felt like it
you became greedy
i became needy

needy // *Besos*-C.A. Gomez

you would stroke the hair on my vagina
but then you started to pull it
wanting it to come off
destroying the vines that protected my temple in the first place

vines // *Besos* -C.A. Gomez

why are you here today

my eyes struggled to keep focus until she called out my name.
from the ugliness of the makeup—she saw freshness as each tear
rolled down my face—there is a kind of beauty
to that

she quietly said again, *why are you here today*

i thought that making an appointment would make me slightly
better
but in truth, i felt defeated, each answer i gave received a careless
shrug
she softened her eyes, and told me we could sit in silence
we learned how to communicate with our eyes
i knew that deep down my head was an unsafe neighborhood to
walk alone
so i had her walk with me
only fifteen minutes left

i pulled out a razor from my bag

can i please dispose of this here

she wore a look of concern

therapy // *Besos*-C.A. Gomez

how is it easy for you to call a body ugly
this is where your soul rests

where it gives you legs to feel this earth
where you rest your palms into mine and i carry your pain

when you say ugly
just remember that this is the same body

that you indulged, kissed, and spoke endless love yous—yet you still
find a way to call it ugly,

i answered

answers // *Besos*-C.A. Gomez

i even wish you well

you   // *Besos*-C.A. Gomez

it was easier for you to
cast blames like fire
rather than admitting
you were wrong
or that my feelings
were actually hurt

blames   // *Besos*-C.A. Gomez

the greatest loss
is when someone
takes your voice
and transforms
it into their echo

echo // *Besos*-C.A. Gomez

the nights reflect our relationship
mysterious and brief

lover // *Besos* -C.A. Gomez

the way you left
told me everything
i needed to know
disregarding how i feel
if we ever bump into each other
the city must not know
to the city we are strangers passing
the secret we decided to keep from the world
because you chose this
it's not us anymore

strangers // *Besos*-C.A. Gomez

each conversation i remember
we began with honesty
why couldn't we finish with it

honesty // *Besos*-C.A. Gomez

i agreed to go back to you
many times
because each version
hit me like perpetual anesthesia
you said you'd change
and i'd forget the past
back and forth
this was us
the storyline
until i drew the line

storyline   // *Besos-*C.A. Gomez

i made a graceful exit to something that outgrew me
closure was not the answer i needed from you
because i didn't want to place myself
in a situation with recycled toxic behavior
the closure may or may not ever come
leaving was the safest option for
my mental health

closure // *Besos*-C.A. Gomez

commitment to rest and movement
tenders the soul
allowing for yourself
to feel thankful and at peace
this balance creates
healthy and strong energy management

energy // *Besos*-C.A. Gomez

my eyes show strength
when you decide
to splash lemon
into them
trying to blind me

lemon // *Besos*-C.A. Gomez

is my voice music you listen to
and the melody that
constantly repeats in your mind
when you stare at the moon
from endless sleepless nights

melody // *Besos*-C.A. Gomez

my heart became an antique to you

you stored it on your shelf

dusting it gently

wrapping it in a cloth

then placing it on the ground

to step on with your foot

but even through

all the cracks

i continued to patch

the pieces together

because that's how

naturally strong the heart is

antique // *Besos*-C.A. Gomez

i am the sunflower
you are attracted to
placing soil in my field
watering me
underestimating
my strength
your darkness
is the shadow
behind me

sunflower // *Besos*-C.A. Gomez

your heart thinks of me
without its permission
but your ego
won't admit it

miss me // *Besos*-C.A. Gomez

i was the museum of art
you had free entrance into
the visuals you saw
became too much for you
seeing my growth
made you uncomfortable
instead of encouraging it
you walked away
leaving the dirt from
your footsteps on my
floor for me to view

museum // *Besos*-C.A. Gomez

insecurities are rooted
and nourished from the fears
that developed from the trauma
it changes us, but will not end us
i take a moment to breathe, cry,
and feel everything that i've
had to keep shut for so long

insecurities // *Besos*-C.A. Gomez

i lost all respect when you
called my mama
the woman who
welcomed you to her home
ugly
a woman who is dead
you called ugly
in order to get back at me

she welcomed you // *Besos*-C.A. Gomez

Besos-50

to hear you say

i'm sorry i hurt you

does not serve me
any happiness
it places me
in a state of
the cruel memories
when i've worked
so hard to outgrow them

to hear you say // *Besos*-C.A. Gomez

the kiss from your lips
draws me back to
our first kiss
back in my room
after some pep rally
we were seventeen
and you made
my heart go
bidi bidi
i lost my heart
that night
thinking i could
fall in love

fall in // *Besos*-C.A. Gomez

RECOLLECTION

mama
despite her illness
stretched dollars
like you do clothes
keeping the roof over our heads
protecting us with all she had

mama
held onto hope for you to come around
my sibling and i never understood why she continued to love you
i would like to believe there was once love there
in stories
marriage was all about love
yet we saw fear, anger, and financial struggles
every year we seemed to be poorer
both of you were water and oil
a pair that didn't work
but created us
leaving us at our demise
your reasons unfolded more and more lies
which became relevant in my eyes
i reminisce on the stress
and her crying out

our life is not fair, and it will never be

i wish i would've thanked her more
because she made miracles out of her heartache

parents // *Besos*-C.A. Gomez

the last goodbyes are never predicated
and sometimes are never even said
but who knew she was going to pass
i would've loved
to share her last laughs
and hugs
to say *thank you*
one last time
because all i vividly remember is the decay
and the frozen bits of time my eyes and her body met

last goodbyes // *Besos*-C.A. Gomez

i came out of a woman who was a latina
whose mother is latina
this is a reminder of how powerful
and ever-growing
we are
and what the future hermanas will continue to be
looking in the mirror i like what i see
because i'm grounded from
various women who know how to fight
and endure the struggle
one woman
coming to america
barely knowing a few english words
hi or *yes*
were the two words that got her by
as abuela learned
mama experienced the same thing
in school
just nodding
finding a place to belong
these women
raising children
became their priority
leaving their dreams second
nuestras madres están cansadas
pero they have shit to do
that's how these women are
la vida es tough
pero so are these women

spanglish // *Besos*-C.A. Gomez

mi abuelita es una mujer fuerte

a mother's worst horror
is when your child dies
before you

mama was abuelita's whole world
mama was a special child, she was abuelita's first real friend
in this country
before anyone else, it was just her and mama
abuelita would come home from work
and see mama waiting to be picked up
to get rootbeer floats and talk about their day
as mama grew older, abuelita experienced
mama's marriage and sickness
through it all they held on together for support
calling each day, eating breakfast everyday
present during mama's hospital visits
praying each day for mama's survival
abuelita never let go of mama's hand
and mama loved her mother unconditionally until her very last
breath

abuelita // *Besos*-C.A. Gomez

Día de Los Muertos is one of our most special holidays
we remember and celebrate the lives of our loved ones
who left a trademark in our hearts
we gather together building la ofrenda
with photos, pan dulce, flowers,
and much more
their photos comfort us
as we look into their eyes
they reach our soul

they say:

remember me
though i might be gone
we'll be reunited again
this is not goodbye
my voice and memories
are forever in your heart
to constantly replay
when you feel lonely

remember me
though i might be gone
our love is everlasting
and a treasure
let me wipe your tears
and mend your heart
death cannot keep us apart
because i'll be waiting for you

to embrace you in my arms again

Día de Los Muertos allows us to
share stories and traditions
because
remembrance never dies

la ofrenda // *Besos*-C.A. Gomez

my grieving period will never end
because when i am at my lowest moments
i feel alone like how my mother was with her thoughts

grief // *Besos*-C.A. Gomez

i gave you my heart because i starved for love
to replace the loss
you became my treatment
for my grieving
tangled through the words you used
thinking you'd fill the love mama had for me
i allowed your control and jealousy
to dominate my mind
thinking that no one else would ever want me
because i was so broken

broken heart // *Besos*-C.A. Gomez

my home became many places
and faces in my lifetime
it wasn't always the same
house or apartment we lived in,
but was the struggle my family
and i ventured through together
it was always about us three
because no matter how hard
the situation got
we reminded one another of the
love and strength
we carried as a unit
and that was a home that could never be taken away

562 (area codes) // *Besos*-C.A. Gomez

we didn't have money,
but kindness to give even to our enemies

enough // *Besos*-C.A. Gomez

biological family
is essential like water
they offer us life or drown us

biological family // *Besos*-C.A. Gomez

we held onto grace and faith
as sufficient resources to survive

resources // *Besos*-C.A. Gomez

when my father would
go in and out from prison
he taught us how to live without him
during our visits
he'd tell me
that recovery was hard
because drugs and theft
were the two things that
presented themselves
as a mean for survival
drugs comforted him
when no one would send letters back
when he *was* out
we suggested therapy
but he felt that it was pointless
the machismo in him
rejected to get in touch with his feelings
because in his world it was be tough or get shot
he told me one time,

i know you hate me, you want me dead, and everytime i try to kill myself it never works

i don't hate nor love him
one thing did become clear to me
it was always about *him*
never once did he
think about the entire family he could've had
but he left it all behind

all about you // *Besos*-C.A. Gomez

the fixation of our bodies
starts at a very young age
i was given permission at thirteen to shave my legs
being latina
my hair laid thick and pretty
like a rose bush
planted
in this garden it created
body grooming came in seasons,
during winter it was okay not to shave,
but in summer hairy legs were looked at
the desperation to shave back then
compares to viewing the scale
it took me so long to actually smile in the mirror
without finding things to hate about my body
if i can go back in time to see my younger self
i'd hold her tight
to tell her how brave and beautiful she is
when i gathered the courage to reclaim my own body
i was able to nurture and pay attention to my mental health
my body did not become someone's blog post
to comment on anymore
my body is ever-changing
my body has hair
my body is mine

beauty standards // *Besos*-C.A. Gomez

starving myself doesn't fix the root of my problem

starvation // *Besos*-C.A. Gomez

my relationship with food is complicated
when life hits me with the worst
the will to eat or persist binges
casts a dark shadow over me
food either angered me or comforted me

food // *Besos*-C.A. Gomez

my body might look normal on the outside
but you don't know of all the battle scars
that i have throughout my temple
it has been destroyed many times
and i am the warrior that restores
it all

latina princess // *Besos*-C.A. Gomez

buckets full of water
balloon fight
my body dances for the sun
my face gleams as my smile sparkles
our backyard transformed into a beach
a place where all the neighborhood kids ran wild
this ought to be for free
  free
  in
  the
  sun
kids unite creating memories
girls and boys of color
splash
  splash
    splash
water splashes on our face
music plays from some guy's ipod nano with a cup over it
at war we are when the water guns come out
girls versus boys
las chicas contra los chicos
water balloons are our grenades
as one splatters on my back
my body falls to the grass
my eyes close not too tight,
so i can hear the outcome of who won
one of the neighborhood girls
brings me a sonic icecream pop
we begin to rant about

the struggles of feeling lonely at school
not understanding the school drama
we went to different districts
and every summer we made it count in fear of one of us moving away
as we got older things changed
people moved
yet you never forget the neighborhood kids you grew up with

summers of 2010-2015 // *Besos*-C.A. Gomez

we are a circle of strength
we may not have everything,
but together we are everything we need
te quiero mucho y el mundo es mi familia

el mundo es mi familia // *Besos*-C.A. Gomez

i never knew about mama's adoption
until her passing
she never mentioned her birth father
it was when i saw in a yearbook
the last name *claudio*
where an untold past unfolded
learning the history of mama's origin
learning of our puerto rican side as well

family tree // *Besos*-C.A. Gomez

mama was blessed and born out of the womb
of mi abuelita
together at heart and never apart
abuela met a man
that saw mama as his own daugther
she was cherished, loved, and wanted

abuelo // *Besos*-C.A. Gomez

abuela:

*I've been working all my life
since I was fifteen years-old
and came to this country*

*I'm tired to be in this world
I feel so useless
I feel like I'm bothering everyone
I just want to be with my daughter*

abuela // *Besos*-C.A. Gomez

mama loved my father
and she saw him as the love of her life
she defended him even from abuela

days before the wedding:

mija, please don't marry him please don't – abuela

pero, mami i love him – mama

night before the wedding:

mija, don't go through this, it's a mistake – abuela

he's a good man, trust me – mama

there's something that doesn't sit right with me mija, something is telling me – abuela

mami, the wedding is tomorrow – mama

i don't care about the money, i care about you, do you really believe in this – abuela

yes i do – mama

the wedding day:

mama's wedding was a dream

her beautiful dress and veil
were perfect
her favorite color purple
was worn by her bridesmaids
everything she always wanted
the love
the start of a new life ahead
as the couple finished their vows
church bells rang
the couple left for the limo
at the venue
people awaited the married couple
no where to be found

then on the news...

local married couple in car crash

those were my parents

the car accident reflected
the relationship
a sudden impact
full of obstacles

wedding day // *Besos*-C.A. Gomez

besos

can be so beautiful

besos, something to remember

un beso entre dos personas diferentes de mundos diferentes

cuando los besas revela su alma y el peso que llevan

besos

can be so toxic

they will stain your lips and live in your body forever

un beso entre dos personas diferentes de mundos diferentes

cuando los besas revela su alma y el peso que llevan

besos // *Besos*-C.A. Gomez

i saw a grown man's naked body
at a very young age
when my father would get
very drunk
he would lie on the floor
soaking in his sweat
and the smell of
alcohol
whiskey eyes is all i remember
vividly
the shot of them looking at me
made me feel uncomfortable
one time i went downstairs
and saw my father lying
on the floor naked
he did nothing
but laid in his filth
saying how he was a horrible person
father, husband, and son
wanting to die
my sibling yelled
and threw a towel on him
covering my eyes and holding me
this is a memory that comes to mind
from time to time
we never told mama
we were too scared
we knew this would break her heart even more

a grown man // *Besos*-C.A. Gomez

when i was little, it was nothing but arroz con frijoles, i knew of nothing else, but my plate needed to be clean finish your food or you will go to hell, abuela said, god refuses entrance to heaven for those who waste food, how could we disobey abuela...

    as you're younger you reflect on
    the religious fables from abuela
    you wonder if these are real or harsh
    you pray, eat, and listen

    the fear instilled in you
    will allow you to appreciate the food
    you have in that moment
because who knows when your next meal will be

    arroz con frijoles is the fuel
    and the meal i always cherish
    because at times that's all we had

    when bills and rent had to be paid
    with little to spare
    arroz con frijoles is what we had

arroz con frijoles // *Besos*-C.A. Gomez

learning the english language
is something i am still understanding
ever since i was little
writing was something i loved,
but it was never easy for me
papers with barely passing grades
struck me harder than lighting
because i wanted to write *correctly*
so badly
in the third grade
i went to young writer's camp
in long beach
kids wrote short stories, poems,
and sci-fi
at the age of eight
i was already criticizing myself
because i felt that my entries
didn't belong there
i felt that all the other kids were great
then there was me
with grammar mistakes
misplacing commas
and misusing words
as i grew older
i aimed to learn english
mi abuela learned
mi mama learned
so why couldn't i
my tongue felt elastic

as it craved and stretched
itself for knowledge
being a brown little girl
english was a river
i rowed my boat on
to travel many obstacles
when many saw me as nothing
i applied to college
when many didn't think i'd get in
because of the personal statement
i got accepted to the university of california, riverside
with a degree in creative writing
when many people said creative writing is not a real major
i published *this* book
i'm thankful for my education
because it cultivated hope and courage
motivation and determination are beautiful tools to life
they are the recipe to dreaming big

english // *Besos*-C.A. Gomez

i was eleven when i got my period
and i cried for days
puberty for us is much more than facial hair,
a tone change, and a growth sprit
a period meant
in society's eyes that i am no longer
a child
i am someone who can produce a human form
a child who sometimes got stared at
a child with developing boobs and hips
and grown men noticed
growing up living in the fear of rape
i was eleven
and i had to think of these things
and be more cautious
instead of just being a kid
but i told myself that my period
makes me powerful
and i am powerful
and i was eleven

eleven // *Besos*-C.A. Gomez

i bleed out so much each month
but do not die
even when i'm asleep
my blood travels and takes its own tours
look at how powerful i am

period // *Besos*-C.A. Gomez

single parenthood
is like a maze
figuring things out on their own
doubling on the priorities
what good am i
if i can't project
the same strength
shown to me
i was raised by a warrior

young warrior // *Besos*-C.A. Gomez

mama's voice:

even when i'm gone remember my love for you
when someone doesn't understand you, i will
when someone breaks your heart, i'll repair it
when someone fails to love you, think of me and i will come to you

a parent's love // *Besos*-C.A. Gomez

mama's diario:

I wish I was a better mother. I miss him. I need him and want him to heal. He is the father of my kids, my love, my possible soulmate. I hate him for what he's done. I can't handle everything by myself anymore. I don't want to. I feel my body aching and know I won't be without pain much longer. I hate that. I feel cheated and punished. I wish I had something to feel really happy and satisfied about. I guess I'm not a very good person for feeling this way. I know God hears me and knows my heart.

mama's diario // *Besos*-C.A. Gomez

mama's diario:

I'm short money and don't know how I'm going to play out the month. Please Lord guide me as to what to do. Send me the solution I need. I miss him so much. We love each other and what is destroying our marriage is his addiction, Lord help him find all the good things in his heart. Help him to fight his addiction.

mama's diario // *Besos*-C.A. Gomez

Besos-93

EMOTIONAL

the softness of my voice
is poetry to your ears
my noises evoke your body
and stimulate your mind
let's focus on breaking my back
than my heart
i touch your soul
i can be your woman
my love is unlike any other
we can do it on the table
then the bed
having the sheets
covering our silhouette from the sun
to your fingers traveling to my hips
and your face kissing each part of my thigh
your lips are mesmorized and high
your teeth can slowly withdraw my thong
revealing my temple
convoyed and wrapped with vines
you immerse your face
into a world so sensual and magical

woman // *Besos* -C.A. Gomez

you've been on me for so long
finding ways to crumble pieces of yourself in me
so that your presence can linger in my memory
you'd give it to me everyday
saying i love you each time
like wine
i thought our love would mature over time
i worshipped you
through all the times you chose to crumble
any confidence left in me
i just wanted you to love me
and be with me
i refused to take care of myself
and put any faith i had in you

the crumbler // *Besos* -C.A. Gomez

the love isn't real anymore when the intimacy is given to someone else

intimacy // *Besos*-C.A. Gomez

sex with me is so magical

you can't have sex with her then want it from me
you want me to forget the cheating
and move straight into my legs to fix the problem
only for you to get laid
leaving me screwed

sex with me // *Besos* -C.A. Gomez

him

women are worthless
you have no choice
i wanna bone you down
have you slobber on my dong

replaying the text messages and all the tears you brought me
my heart could not take no more
for the times i told you i love you, till this day i regret it

texts // *Besos*-C.A. Gomez

the wetness of my pussy
is not a sign of consent for you to touch me
the wetness of my pussy is a response to many things
anxiety of what might happen to me
to prepare for the rape
and protection so the pain doesn't hurt so much
the wetness of my pussy
is not something for you to claim
the wetness of my pussy
is not consent

bodily reactions // *Besos*-C.A. Gomez

how would you feel
if the one person
you trusted the most
said that all your
progress and feelings
are invalid
the one person you
thought believed in you

the one person // *Besos*-C.A. Gomez

your kisses to me are a drug
yet they don't destroy my memory
it's hard to quit you
even though i know you're not good for me
everytime i see you i don't want to behave
with each kiss i really thought you were good person
but you deceived me just like your kisses did

kisses are a drug // *Besos*-C.A. Gomez

driving alone for the first time
pretending you were there in the passenger seat
what our lives could have been
passing through the sunsets and long roads
each redlight feels forever
the pauses in between makes it hard to not cry
driving alone to a party
pretending to be alright
and fake my way through the night
what you put me through i can't lie
i left for my own sanity
you live in your own vanity
maybe you'll call
and i'll pick up because
i'm so damn emotional

driver's seat // *Besos*-C.A. Gomez

if my vagina could speak
it would say:

grow yourself one to see how painful pounding objects or penises are

a vagina is resilient

a vagina decided to bring you in this world show some respect

my vagina should not be in discussion with what i do with it

a vagina can stretch, transform, and mold it's shape, this is powerful

my pussy hairs are not a problem, mind your own business

my pussy is poetic, it has it's own pair of lips that speaks to my lovers

if my pussy was deep enough it would trap you

vagina // *Besos*-C.A. Gomez

your hands have so much power
i still remember each touch
they laid on this body
cursed to feel
the rape is something unforgettable
but it will not end me

hands // *Besos*-C.A. Gomez

am i the devil
because you can't seem to quit me
maybe you're under my spell
i got delicious taste
and you're in love with my body
or
maybe it's
that your wrongdoings
are resurfacing from hell to the earth
in order to haunt you
does it make you regret it all
i will never forget
as you shouldn't either

devil // *Besos*-C.A. Gomez

men have been inside me
experiencing another lifetime
an old version of me
connected to that person
i have left her a long time ago
losing so much
i gained more for evolving

evolve // *Besos*-C.A. Gomez

mi muerte será el último empujón para que le cuentes a la gente la verdadera historia

estoy esperando // *Besos* -C.A. Gomez

i pretend to finish so that the pain can stop
hearing my silence sounds better to me
than my cry

finish // *Besos* -C.A. Gomez

our fights
those are the hardest to look back on
when it was in the car
the dorm or apartment
you yelled
those words reached the back
of my throat
as i would tear up
you'd tell me to stop
choking on my tears
every little thing i did annoyed you
i felt that it was always my fault
one day you loved me
the next you hated me
our last fight
you held my hands to the chair
as you faced me to yell
then pinned me to the ground
because i was trying to kick you
away from me
our fights
made me extremely paranoid
our fights almost ended me

our fights // *Besos* -C.A. Gomez

they found me on the floor that night
pills scattered everywhere
i'm so glad i heard
we're here...
we're here...
it's gonna be okay...
instead of leaving my body
i told myself to never
go to this state of mind
ever again
no person is
worth ending my life
i am worth so much
more than that

that night // *Besos* -C.A. Gomez

i cry alone
since my body can't provide anything else
words feel impossible since i was told
to keep quiet for so long
before i was able to tell someone
about everything that happened
i turned to the page
to flesh out the pain
that was controlling my body
as the poison bled from
my fingertips
i was given clarity
and i was able to finally speak

clarity // *Besos* -C.A. Gomez

how do you cope with the breakup
do you think there were better ways for us to treat our relationship better
did you tell your friends the truth about our relationship
did you ever find yourself wanting to apologize
do you think i should apologize
why did we need to hide our relationship from your friends
during the day you'd act like you didn't know me
but in closed doors you were up on me
where is your insecurity rooted from
from the times you'd cuddle me close to you
whispering in my ear that you wanted a future
was that ever true
or was that the motive for me to keep quiet
did our relationship teach you anything
what was the reason you decided to degrade me
with every action or word i said
you'd call me stupid and hopeless
do you still see me as someone poor
living on the street with their poetry
do you really think my voice isn't strong
enough to reach others
were there any toxic traits you saw from me
could i have been a better partner
why did you think i could never survive financially by myself
why did my life depend on your decisions
could you sense my fear and did that entice you
comparing me to other people did you think
that would make me your ideal partner

when i left did your fear come from
actually missing me or missing the control

i tried to keep us together
i wasn't gonna text your mom about us or tell her about your behavior
you're too much of a coward to confront the problem
you're too much of a coward to admit to her that you cheated
why did you think isolating myself from my friends and family was a solution
i know you didn't have the best relationship with my family
but who gave you the right to say you'd rather see them dead
who are you to judge
who are you to judge my sibling for their disability
what kind of evil are you
tell me what kind of fucked up drug you're on, so maybe i can understand
masking yourself from everyone with who you really are
from the point i tried to stand up for myself
you'd shut it down and tell everyone i was crazy
since when did you understand the definition of crazy
i want to know why you decided to take out all your insecure emotions on me

how long do you think i'd realize you wouldn't change
from the moment you grabbed a razor
i was in the shower alone, you came in
shaved my vagina and peed on me
while i cried

how is humiliation refreshing to you
was the urination to put me in my place
because of those moments
it made it hard to shower
i feared that someone would invade my space like you did

i wonder if your mother will ever know of how you truly spoke to me
i will reminisce on these questions once more
will she be able to still call you her son
why is it that women who are being oppressed seem funny to you
tell me why
tell me how that is supposed to make me feel
why was i afraid of you for so long
tell me, self, tell me
what gave you the right to act out your depression onto me
was i just some useless punching bag
what is the real reason you cheated on me
i wonder if you would have liked it
if i found some random guy
fucked him just to spite you
you wouldn't have liked it
you would've felt broken and torn to the core,
but i'm not that type of bitch, yet you are to me
why the fuck do you think i'd be cool with it then
i don't know why you decided to hurt me
what did you really think of this relationship
was it just convenient for you
who did you tell about the cheating first

i need to know
who told you it was ok to treat women the way you did with me
it is not ok
who gave you the right to make me believe that i had to say *yes* all the time
tell me now
when did you first love me
when did i first make you cry
was it as painful as mine
where will you go now
please don't come near me
where will your kisses go to next
how come i thought you would kill me if i left you
how come i was afraid of you for so long
how come

questions to him // *Besos* -C.A. Gomez

dear 21,
are you truly happy...
do you see yourself in a place where you feel growth...

dear 21,
i want you to know that you are a woman of color and should be proud
you will master the spanish language in due time
the important thing is that you are practicing and learning now
those who continue to doubt your ability are the ones that will be seeing you from their phone screens
it is normal to cry, to feel frustration, but it does not make you weak

dear 21,
you receive unconditional love around you
you might feel like you're alone now, but know that there are people out there experiencing the same thing as you, and the world is waiting for you to meet them
when you meet them, they will truly understand and accept you for who you truly are
you are a woman with lots of knowledge to share
you are a woman with lots of love to give

dear 21,
your self-expression is valid
every single fashion choice you make, wear it confidently
ignorant people are the ones who are a few steps behind you not in front of you
your passion for your hobbies was never a flaw to begin with

dear 21,
you are a human being and deserve to be treated like one

dear 21 // *Besos*-C.A. Gomez

he doesn't love you
my inner self told me
after finally realizing
all the pain
and all the discomfort
he really just
emotional abuses me

emotional abuse // *Besos*-C.A. Gomez

you want to turn off my memories
and start all over, but that's not fair to me

memories // *Besos*-C.A. Gomez

attraction is mysterious, it doesn't always make sense, but there's this magnetism pulling our forces together

magnetism // *Besos*-C.A. Gomez

graduating college during 2020
degreed and broke
on the floor i layed
trying to hold onto any hope i had left
my air mattress popped
rent due
the floor seemed to engulf me
i felt that you and many others were right
i was a broke poet
i was so broke
i wonder if anyone thought of me
i was so broke
i couldn't even pay attention to writing
every night i submerged my face into
in my pillow
i remembered days would get better
and your words would not run my life
just because i am broke right now
doesn't mean i will
grant a poor state of mind
to dictate the rest of my life
being broke
gave me more motivation
to fight for my dreams
and invest in myself
degreed
i plant a seed
that can feed me a plentiful path
for those who pursue their passion

i know it can be tempting to reread
the college manual
and question our major
but we know
lots of love for something comes lots of labor

degreed and broke // *Besos* -C.A. Gomez

some months were really hard
my mind and body
were starved
wanting to eat
but paying rent came first
so i can have somewhere
else to sleep rather than my car

how i felt about myself:

i am so ugly
i am so moody
i am so done...

eating // *Besos* -C.A. Gomez

it is not healthy or helpful
when people feel the need
to provide unnecessary
comments about our bodies
we shouldn't lean into them
even if they come from our families
because it will trigger
that inner voice we've tried so hard to silence
the voice activates and makes us
forget about all the hard work
we've put in and the recovery

recovery // *Besos* -C.A. Gomez

recovery to self is an ongoing journey, you're always changing and growing

journey // *Besos* -C.A. Gomez

i loved you more than life itself

unhealthy love // *Besos*-C.A. Gomez

him

*you're being too much of a bitch
i can see your pussy hairs
those stretch marks though*

stop it

texts // *Besos*-C.A. Gomez

sometimes the apologies come
when they are not needed nor wanted
but time likes to play
every second watches
every fiber of my being
and strikes me

time // *Besos*-C.A. Gomez

you stutter when i ask you certain questions
it's okay i get the message
you want to lie
and i'm supposed to comply
you don't care that my feelings are hurt
teach me how to be like you
so i can learn how to not give a fuck
but it's not worth it
it's time for goodbye
and let karma have the last laugh
say thank you to your mom for me on my behalf

over it // *Besos*-C.A. Gomez

ending things before you end me
alone and brave is what i am
and not afraid to die alone

alone // *Besos*-C.A. Gomez

am i prepared
because falling into you
means falling out of him
and is my heart ready for that next step
to not compare
to not feel insecure
like clothes
this person
will now wear me, but will they tear me
am i a perfect fit
or are there loose ends that need to be patched
or discovered
alterations...
i hadn't thought of that

new relationship // *Besos*-C.A. Gomez

WORLD

the sun
fatigued, drained, and tired
still rises for the earth
every single day
so where are you

earth // *Besos*-C.A. Gomez

to you i am like water
you can't live without me,
i
provide life to those who
cherish me
the taste of me evokes
your thoughts and memories
my water pulses you
every moment is your last
you fall into my river
i drown you
you're with me now
there's nothing you can do
we drown and drown
dragging each other to the end
no one will save you

river // *Besos*-C.A. Gomez

remembering that this body
is rooted from
various generations
of a beautiful community
who fed me with water
clear as crystal
wanting me to grow
spreading the roots
i sprouted out from

roots // *Besos*-C.A. Gomez

i longed for you
to feel the same pain i felt
but that wouldn't change anything
it would make me into a person
no better than you

thoughts // *Besos*-C.A. Gomez

snipping all of our photos
i spent the entire night
making a fire of my own
igniting my soul

fire // *Besos* -C.A. Gomez

working overtime
my body barely touches the sheets
waking up so single and falling asleep the same
never felt so good
being alone gave me a new perspective
not used to feeling this way
and that is comfortable without you
no matter what obstacle i take on next
i will protect my soul over anything else

breakup // *Besos*-C.A. Gomez

i am not ashamed to start over, i deserve to

new beginnings // *Besos*-C.A. Gomez

there are moments
where i ask my therapist

will mental illness end me

neglect and abandonment
is not something i can easily separate from my past

what are you supposed to do
when it gets to this point

the real sad thing is that
i can be healing, hurting,
and wanting to succumb all at the same time
i don't know why

the discussions // *Besos*-C.A. Gomez

use this time to
exercise your energy
in people who
put in the same love
and effort you do
outgrowing friendships
is normal
especially the ones you
have to constantly chase
these type of relationships
cannot complete you
people change, and so do you
there's nothing wrong with that

outgrow // *Besos*-C.A. Gomez

those who left you during difficult times
attempt to reprise their role into your life
they paint you a perfect picture

take a moment

why do they deserve a full-position into your life
when they declared you as a second option to begin with
to be candid
you were taken for granted

candid // *Besos*-C.A. Gomez

you can love someone so much
and it may not look like anything is wrong,
but it's important to reflect on these
questions

why am i really here
do i love them or
do i want to help them

the only person who can do that
is themselves

you're only winding up
yourself to take a long
ride with an impossible
never ending road

quarantine with you // *Besos*-C.A. Gomez

i wonder if you can hear my voice through the texts
i know it breaks your heart
when i remember him
but this is something i have to do
with all the growth you've seen
there is a dark hole that has yet to be covered
i love you for loving me through this
after all i've been through
i do my best to leave the trauma in these poems
i know it breaks your heart
to see me crying
and remembering the pain he caused me
instead of a memory
i hope he becomes a ghost
something i cannot see or feel anymore

ghost // *Besos*-C.A. Gomez

dreaming in the bathtub
me with no makeup
bubbles swarming everywhere
imaging that the bubbles are your lips
this feels like the closest pleasure to your body on mine
the warmth holds me like you do
making this a regular to survive the absence you give me
saying i love you on the phone
hits more
i just miss you
i'm the earth
and you're outer space
can our love endure the universe

long distance relationship // *Besos*-C.A. Gomez

let my kisses fly to you like a butterfly
let it tour all of your sweet spots
until your lips sever from mine
will you kiss me just a little longer
the separation feels like forever

mariposa // *Besos*-C.A. Gomez

my grandmother and i share the same pain
praying to god
hoping to see our loved one once more
will the world allow us to be reunited
mother, grandmother, and granddaughter
i know when i cry
mi abuela is crying too
we smile in front of others
while the anxiety rests comfortably throughout our body
i imagine
my mother
mi mami
in the heavens above
holding a globe
watching the turmoil spill over
embracing the globe close to her eyes
as the tears rejuvenate our soul to continue just a bit longer
our love is one of the same
keeping us strong to fight
giving us the air to breathe
our language is how we communicate
a beautiful language shared among many others
from the heaven to earth
through the stars and sky
lies a bridge from us to her
my mother
mi mami
carries the world in this globe
waiting for our time to be reunited

her world // *Besos*-C.A. Gomez

we are not broken
to be broken
meant we created something
and what did we create
when we pretend to not
know one another
with every turning leaf
and changing season
our bond is always at fall
never hitting spring
our relationship
has not begun
for when it does
the fire we bury deep
will warm our hearts
with love
instead of rumors,
gossip, and chisme
this rapid fire
no one admits to
gets out of control
just like our emotions
when we consistently
ignore one another
a fire can bring light
to something broken
if we both ignite it

fire // *Besos*-C.A. Gomez

when someone disrespects you the first time
they are given
the opportunity to lie
to you again in only a different way
over and over
until you end
your forgiveness towards them
many will envy you
while only a few will
celebrate you
open with your heart
but lead with your mind

heart and mind // *Besos*-C.A. Gomez

with a world ever-changing
we still live in fear of racism
and people still wanting to control
women's bodies
these people claim to protect children
yet we see them in danger
in the eyes of human trafficking
the lack of health-care and therapy
two shots is all it takes
to kill not only one but many
children who dreamed of
pursuing an education
i have family members who are teachers
they are hanging by the thread
in this era of shootings
having a hard time finding joy
in what is the most respectable job
because our teachers are our second parents
or simply are *our* parents to the ones we've never had
children, teachers, and parents suffer mentally
yet the gun
holds more power
how about taking time
to make useful changes
surviving a day
bears our minds
because we don't know
if we'll live to see the next day

changes // *Besos*-C.A. Gomez

to all the women i've met
or will meet in this lifetime
thank you for your intelligence and bravery
in the midst of this world
we are warriors
fighting battles everyday
when we are catcalled,
harassed, and ridiculed
each year seems like a new battle
we with uteruses
are yet failed again
in fear of regressing towards something worse
repeating history's mistakes
in a country
where guns hold more rights and respect
than we do
and now we are facing
the one where again
our bodies are the topic
under the toxic tongue
of those who feel
that the girl
who wants to
find promise in her decisions
to her own body
can't
we stand here today
with courage
we can change history around us

courage is contagious
and as a force
we are serving for our loved ones,
and the future generations ahead
there is no limit to what we can do

uterus // *Besos*-C.A. Gomez

safety for all women and LGBTQIA+ people is so essential
because we are a large percentage of
anger, hate, and control
when i'm walking alone on the street
and i see another woman
i look out for her too
especially when we're walking the same path
because we're possible prey
of those who hunger
and view our bodies as meat
plotting to skin us to the bone
i glance back
one earbud in
with pepperspray on duty
we're in this together

safety // *Besos*-C.A. Gomez

our country will never reveal
how we women are the main fuel
because we are the ones capable of life
the pussy speaks volume in its power
this country
continues to stifle on us women from our potential
we are leaders, educators, and empowerers
we lead by example and not by fear
hope and grit is our secret weapon
we are never tired
and will never rest
remember this
we are fearless

fearless // *Besos*-C.A. Gomez

i would like my body to deteriorate
peacefully, and not from your words
it is a country that has conquered
endless battles and was birthed
by the creator herself, and i
will not allow you to be my
destroyer
i have too much
to learn from the women in
my bloodline and pass onto the
little girls forward that have eyes
of hope

legacy // *Besos*-C.A. Gomez

i will honor my mind and body
to continue through this life of mine

oath // *Besos*-C.A. Gomez

prioritizing feeling safe
protecting my emotional energy
ignoring you
and loving me more

balanced priorities // *Besos*-C.A. Gomez

surrounded by a powerful force
that are my fellow hermanas y mujeres
hits different than any
other relationship
we become united

womanhood // *Besos*-C.A. Gomez

as a collective we can change the world

collective // *Besos*-C.A. Gomez

art
just like our path
shouldn't be compared
to other people's progress
when art is created
from the emotion
and devotion
that is our experience
art is different
people's lives are different
don't timestamp
yourself

art // *Besos*-C.A. Gomez

the experiences you've fought for
been through, and taught to others
let them be the lessons
that galvanize
a positive impact
i'm here to advise
for you to rise
because you are *so* wise
our anxieties and fears
try their best to downplay our success
thinking we are not good enough
when we are capable of making
our dreams happen
we are so intelligent,
dedicated, and loved
time to romanticize these affirmations

romanticize // *Besos*-C.A. Gomez

you say you want to be friends
yet the moment you appear in my life
you create drama scattering it everywhere
like if it were the season of fall
with each leaf touching the ground
for your feet to crush them
god brought you in and out my life for a reason
the same being that
god created one face for you
yet you decide to wear two
thinking i'd be a fool
self-respect is my religion
i recognize my value and time
not letting you or anyone else trample me ever again

self-respect // *Besos*-C.A. Gomez

you are judged for being real
yet *they're* loved for being fake
the wit of these words
is like a coin
whatever hand is tossed
that's how we're seen
when the world is ever changing
so are we
we're gonna make mistakes
we're gonna learn
because that's the process

the process // *Besos*-C.A. Gomez

it is so difficult
having a mental illness
that some do not understand completely
and many stereotype it as a cleanliness disorder
when obsessive compulsive disorder is much more than that
to the ones suffering with this, i stand here
since i was seven the disorder emerged
like a never ending vortex
it did start with cleanliness
i had to wash my hands 17 times a day and the only person
who never judged me was my mama
she was the one who gave me small sanitizers
to help me throughout grade school
losing friendships or being fun made of
because no one understood
and found it easier to judge
and as i got older the cleanliness died down
and shifted to my mind
obsessing over thoughts like
will people like me
am i capable of making friends
why can't i look like them
living in my thoughts
having them dictate every fiber of my being
looking fine on the outside
but screeching from the inside
these thoughts will shuffle
and form into different species
in my brain

that feed off my joy
and dive into my depression
struggling with both
it makes it hard to sleep
my thoughts go up and down
as i follow my heartbeat
mental illness can take you
high up or down low
but as i've gone through therapy
and with all the love and support from my life
i don't let mental illness be the problem
it is something that has made me stronger
it makes me a brave and powerful woman
to share my mental health journey is not easy
my vulnerability is poured out to you
like a cup of tea
you can drink it or throw it on me
and let it burn
to reveal all of me that i gave to you
only for you to judge
but i can't and won't let
judgement dictate my life
i stand here to speak about this battle
to express how proud i am of myself
to be here today
mental illness is on a spectrum
from the trauma and loss
i've dealt with
there are good and bad days

and i live to survive each damn day

mental health journey // *Besos*-C.A. Gomez

hug those close to you
squeeze them tight
we don't know what someone
is going through
suffering isn't always visible
pain is taxing
it is
an enigma
when pain comes for you or someone else
our love
our embrace can be a light
to shine through someone's suffering

enigma // *Besos*-C.A. Gomez

normalize taking breaks in friendships
both individuals deserve to restore

friendships // *Besos*-C.A. Gomez

i was a victim of
sexual and emotional abuse
when people you trust
don't initially believe you
i know it can be easy to fall
into a dark place
because the initial response
lingers in your mind
and reveals everything to you
but i want to stress to you
that you are never alone
and you can get through this
because you are so powerful
and so brave for speaking up
your voice and circle of strength
will always be with you

the initial response // *Besos*-C.A. Gomez

i tell them i'm not home
using that do not disturb feature
trying to focus on myself
i'm good on my own
reflecting on my goals
doing my best to make them happen
learning to keep myself happy

disconnection // *Besos*-C.A. Gomez

i have chosen to walk away
dislike my boundaries, not my problem,
but how do you expect me to have you around
tell me
how

how // *Besos*-C.A. Gomez

my patience is not like the sun
even though it might seem like it
it will not always be there to shine through
i rise, but i'm also tired
and there will be the day where i can't be the sun for you anymore

sun // *Besos*-C.A. Gomez

seeking validation from others
will not make you happy

validation // *Besos*-C.A. Gomez

living life always comes with
new things to venture
nerves are part of it
replacing one anxiety with another
but growing from it

dark truths // *Besos*-C.A. Gomez

compliments are much more than just physical
they are when you tell people
how you admire their honesty
thanking them for their positive impact
thanking them for their energy
thanking them for giving you a safe space

thankful // *Besos*-C.A. Gomez

does the kindness quote you post on instagram reflect back to you

post // *Besos*-C.A. Gomez

feeling unsafe starts at a young age
when you feel afraid to disagree or speak up
people who invalidate you constantly
expect you to stay a people-pleaser
let me tell you
you're much more than that

people-pleaser // *Besos*-C.A. Gomez

a balance where you are able
to vent about your joy and hardships
in life is healthy

both // *Besos*-C.A. Gomez

the woman who struggled in me
she is a side of me that has given me beautiful poetry
she is not a problem, she is apart of me
i love her and accept her

i love her // *Besos*-C.A. Gomez

living through integrity

integrity // *Besos*-C.A. Gomez

him

you expect everything to be in little bite sized pieces, already chewed up
for you
you never take the time to just think
i don't get what's so fucking hard

i wanted an apology from you for so long, but for what
your words aren't worth it to me

texts // *Besos*-C.A. Gomez

can you imagine
a scenario of me being
immuned from your dark magic
the magician you were
the spells you put on me
wore off as i chose myself
for the first time
you could never imagine
me cutting off the strings
you stitched to my body
to control me
because control was always your goal
and you could never imagine me
leaving
but you don't have to
because it is the reality
i don't care about you anymore
i don't care for you anymore
i don't want you in my blood anymore
no need for you to apologize
it's all good
i'm healing without you
you, wanted me to grab your hand
as i fell from your grasp
i said *no*
you asked why we couldn't work
immuned from your spells
i used potions on myself
to heal and survive

and leave you forever

immune // *Besos*-C.A. Gomez

CROWN

tus ojos me miran
mi cuerpo se disuelve dentro del suelo
estoy plantado

mi aroma es dulce,
pero si arrancas mis pétalos
haré sangrar tu mano

hablas de mí
te burlas de mí
tienes una adicción al azúcar

sigue comiendo
soy morena y bonita
es hora de mostrar al mundo lo que está orgullosa latina puede hacer

azúcar morena // *Besos*-C.A. Gomez

the crackling noise you hear
from me walking down the stage
will break you
knowing i stand tall
where i belong
no one can
shut me off
anymore

inspire // *Besos*-C.A. Gomez

there's so much to you mija
they told me
respira y escucha
let your presence bring attention
break barriers and ascend

self-discovery // *Besos*-C.A. Gomez

forever thankful that i gathered up the courage to take you out of my life
what a gain

gain // *Besos* -C.A. Gomez

i remind myself everyday of how powerful i am
the way i look at myself in the mirror
is something special

mirrors // *Besos*-C.A. Gomez

i am learning to love myself
before i ever have it with anyone else again

self-love // *Besos*-C.A. Gomez

growth deserves to be celebrated not criticized

growth // *Besos*-C.A. Gomez

you gave me so much pain
and here i am making
something out of it
what a win for me
and a lose for you

win // *Besos*-C.A. Gomez

my skin stays glowing
because i stay hydrated
in my own lane

glow // *Besos*-C.A. Gomez

i gave people tlc without an expiration date
i'm learning the lesson to not give my heart away
to some piece of shit
i'm not here to write a false narrative with you
i'm too good for that and much more greedy with my time
if i want something done i depend on me
sitting on my throne
aligning my crown

crown // *Besos*-C.A. Gomez

whenever i'm alone nowadays
the memory of april nineteenth pops up from time to time
never having time to process it
until six years later
no one in the family likes to talk about it
does it make me a bad daughter for not saying one last goodbye
you left for a whole new world
but if i'm going to be honest
with this quarantine your love would have been destroyed
sucked out of your body
leaving you to levitate in the air
possibly you entering your own world was for the best
until then you will remain there
and i shall remain here

conversations with god // *Besos*-C.A. Gomez

i still cry
when i am happy
and have everything
but, deep down
the happiness still doesn't feel real

happiness and truth // *Besos*-C.A. Gomez

everyone take a seat for la lotería
all your tios, tias, y primos
come through
placing uncooked beans
on the pictures
of la rosa, la mano, el mundo
el sol y etc.
you see a new illustration
on your card
labeled
la celeste
her symbol
is poetic and dynamic
she wears eyes of integrity
with red lips
iconic as frida
stylish like selena
la celeste
her eyes speak to you
la poeta
la artista
la autora
a game of chance
a game of poetry
la celeste
represents a driven mujer

la lotería // *Besos*-C.A. Gomez

i'm drawn to your presence
you smile because you feel the same
my heart is yours
to enter into
i immerse myself into yours
a love true from you
from all the others
ours is something
growing and overflowing
with honesty, friendship,
and effort
you are the love that
can slip inside my skin
and plant your kisses
building a home
within me
you are the love that
articulates all my inner
emotions
supporting me through
thick and thin
you are the love that
means so much to me

our love // *Besos*-C.A. Gomez

there is a pulse between us
something heavy we are creating
you have a way with your lips
poetic and dynamic
don't stop, don't stop
this time
i want it and i'll be honest
your hand enters inside me
until your finger cramps up
my bruises heal slowly
by your embrace
your sweet lips
suck on my sweet spots
the head is special
don't stop, don't stop
this is something mesmerizing
nothing feels better than this

don't stop // *Besos*-C.A. Gomez

we lie in bed
the sheets covering half our bodies
your force, so magnetic
draws upwards
i feel the softness of your being
on me
kissing me softly
you see me smile
my eyes still closed
i'm in love
and i'm all in

real love // *Besos*-C.A. Gomez

the smile you give me
is the same curve my back feels
i hear your voice
you're muttering my name
you're wanting more
i'm the brown sugar
your tongue licks
the curves that are my hips
are so natural and beautiful
as they should be
my breasts lay as they should be
they are juicy fruit
to cure your sweet tooth
for the first time i'm not worried
on how i should look
i accept the gift that is my body
the cellulite i tried to hide on my thighs
are stripes of growth
you're in the mood to please me
i open the gateway from the vines
and it feels free

curves // *Besos*-C.A. Gomez

i gathered the courage
to take out the loss words
that drowned from the last
ship i rode
now i can see the sun,
i speak clearly
and hold your hands firmly

i love you // *Besos*-C.A. Gomez

thank you to all the boys i've dated
for showing me parts of myself
i never thought i'd ever see

our relationship taught me
patience and how
to patch up the broken pieces
from my heart

our relationship taught me
that i don't have to be complacent
in situations or people i'm not comfortable with
we were placed in each other's lives for a reason
and a short season
allowing us to experience the deepest
emotions within
from the good and bad

our relationship gave me a new
perspective in what i want
and evoked the courage inside myself
to become stronger
the midst of the heartache might
have felt pivotal
but gave me control of my life again

our relationship taught me
that the breakup was the best
decision for my happiness

and individualism
i am able to open many doors
and opportunities for when i left
or you left
us ending the relationship
allowed me to see the sun
so i can shine along with it
instead of dry into crisps

thank you to all the boys
who broke my heart
you taught me that i
dictate my own happiness
and love for myself

so thank you

thank you to all the boys i've dated // *Besos*-C.A. Gomez

you weren't the one for me
and maybe the next one won't be either
but being alone
doesn't mean i gave up on the idea of love
i am taking time
to protect and refresh my soul
refine my goals and desires
because the love i pour out
must be watered on myself first
before i can pour into
someone else again

pour // *Besos*-C.A. Gomez

my nakedness does not belong to you
it is mine to hold and love

sanctuary // *Besos*-C.A. Gomez

at the age of nineteen
i had my very first gyno appointment
the thing they don't tell you about these
sessions is that it is not quick like a simple shot
or that it would be extremely uncomfortable
unclothed from the bottom
my pussy dry and crumbled
like the leaves that are sucked into a hurricane

my pussy agitated
the tool enters
a cold shudder stuffs itself inside me
it is forceful and a pain like before
i ask the gynecologist to stop
the female nurse giving me water
we continue and i still feel pain
the gynecologist stops and asks

haven't you had a penis in you before

silence stood still between his disgustful mind
and these scared feelings
he starts to continue
tears in my eyes
i kick slowly and the nurse calms me down
he leaves

as i change i think about his question
the fact is that many women besides myself

have unfortunately had a penis inside us
the discomfort of having our consent ignored
made me feel ashamed to have this pussy
the one thing that we squeeze out of
people find a way to harm it
the one thing that men call each other
as an insult when in fact they are nothing of a pussy
to embody the power of pussy is much more than that

changing back into my clothes
wiping my tears
reminding myself that it is not my pussy's fault for being dry
my pussy is dry from that man's presence
from the memory of my ex's penis being as foreign as that tool
cold and hard
the sex was painful
that's all i knew
pain

gynecologist // *Besos*-C.A. Gomez

to reflect
no means no
it is not

are you sure
think about it again
oh i thought we just would

flipping the situation from pleasure to pain
only to be twisted for your own necessities
no means no

no means no // *Besos-*C.A. Gomez

you claim to celebrate women
when we are promoted,
proposed to, or pregnant

but

are you celebrating us
when we have an abortion,
leaving a toxic relationship, or
being a single parent

if you're not doing all of these
then you are simply not celebrating women

you want to understand women
then listen
hear our voice for once

listen // *Besos*-C.A. Gomez

his name still triggers me
even if it's a nice person
i meet from work
or passing by
this name has its
own language
that is difficult for me to unlearn
and it is a fire that finds a way to
flow, change, and grow in me

his name // *Besos*-C.A. Gomez

just because our lips connected doesn't mean our hearts did

linked // *Besos*-C.A. Gomez

wanting your apology will only entice the idea of that we can be in communication again

idea // *Besos*-C.A. Gomez

writing is the only thing that saved me
it became my form of healing

these feelings i held inside
are now fleshed out
my words bring power to me
when i started writing for myself
i finally found my voice

the inner voice // *Besos*-C.A. Gomez

with everything happening in the world
poetry needs to be shared more than ever
these words are meant for everyone
especially for those in their youth
high school seniors, college students,
post graduates
don't let your dreams fall astray

poetry // *Besos*-C.A. Gomez

the voice i have is so powerful
the little poet in me brings herself out from her bubble
letting her words create a bridge for me to walk on
my feet take gentle steps as the words climb onto me
my body is lifted up as the words swirl in my hair like the wind
the soul of my body generates light
words that feed off trauma, happiness, and culture surround me
my eyes become like glass because the little poet in me is in control
little poet, use your voice
move mountains and destroy storms
release peace within yourself
do not let anyone silence you
you are an ever changing spirit
what a thing to be human
creative spirit don't ever stop
little poet, you are the inspiration
the strong force
because little poet
you are me

little poet // *Besos*-C.A. Gomez

thank you to all my friends
for your positive influence in my life
and going the extra mile
when it comes to support
finding true friends
are rare
and they are the gems
that shine with you
our friendship is so precious to me
during hard times
we rely on each other
whether it be talking on the phone
facetiming, getting boba,
binging shows, or sending
cute check-in messages
true friends inspire you
true friends grow with you
true friends love you

love letter to my friends // *Besos*-C.A. Gomez

i will always love
and
never fall into hatred
even when the obstacles
exercise all the bones within
my body
from various broken hearts
to a chain of unfair events
i simply love
to never self-destruct
again
my body was the ticking time bomb
filled with anger and frustration
letting every hour
tick by
as i consume myself in these
form of emotions
feasting through my brain
draining time
not giving one dime
i choose to never
self-destruct again
and to simply love

overcome // *Besos-*C.A. Gomez

degreed
hungry with a dream
if i ain't got no one
at least god believes in me
my experiences turned me into
a thriving queen
traded in my old self-esteem
for something greater
time is on my wrist
focused on
completing my checklist

mala // *Besos*-C.A. Gomez

give yourself many chances to
cleanse your mind
so you can
reach your goals
you set your mind on
don't let anything or anyone
guilt trip you from moving forward
your one life is valuable
and must be cherished

value // *Besos*-C.A. Gomez

when my heart is at rest
i can focus on my breathing
and sleep peacefully
without having nightmares
of you or my fears
because i have finally forgiven
myself from this journey

peace // *Besos*-C.A. Gomez

understanding my journey
by appreciating my worth and blessings
has allowed me to celebrate my life more

celebrate // *Besos*-C.A. Gomez

it is rare that my mind will cast good memories of us ever again

rare // *Besos*-C.A. Gomez

love was the muscle i worked
when i chose to stay with you
from the bitter text messages
to the lies you told
i am done with you
from the lack of tenderness
i received
your love is pain
my hell and heaven on a coin
which side would you show onto me next
every flip turned into some guilt trip
the strength i had to love you
i displayed when i left you

chapter ending // *Besos*-C.A. Gomez

your past self is a beautiful dream
your future self is the harsh reality
and you're not meant to fill
the empty parts of me
i take time to breathe

the wind you try to be
you want to follow in my direction
the storms you try to cast
will not phase me

despite all the storms
i have grown
into a woman
running her own throne

throne // *Besos*-C.A. Gomez

the reason i am who i am today
is because i always go to my true spot
the reason i can directly look at my face
in the mirror is because i'm not hiding
from myself or in anyone else's shadow anymore
this is something that has taken time
i'm not glorifying my past relationships
i'm not asking for pity for losing a parent
i'm asking for you to understand
only to be respectful
and to see how these obstacles
shaped me to the person i am

the reason // *Besos*-C.A. Gomez

listen to the words i have to say
let it sink in and resonate on the experience
i'm not a role model, but a *real model*
a woman of color navigating her twenties,
trying to survive
if i'm playing the role that everything is alright
then i'm not connecting with people, if i stay true
to myself then i'm not bringing anyone down
because i'm being human
i want you to listen and read exactly what i've been through

words from miss gomez // *Besos*-C.A. Gomez

him

i hate you
you left me
you don't want me back
wow, leave me on read

leaving a toxic relationship is a victory, it was time for me to let you go
our abusers train us to be scared and feel crazy
remember you are never alone

texts // *Besos*-C.A. Gomez

ABOUT THE AUTHOR

Celeste Alyssa Gomez is a first time self-publish Latina author. She graduated from the University of California, Riverside with a degree in Creative Writing. She started posting poetry online on Instagram and selling poems at pop-up events. During the pandemic, she shifted to Instagram Live to host poetry workshops and open mics for artists to share their voice. Through her poetry, Celeste expresses how the themes of grief, love, abandonment, empowerment, and culture contribute to her healing process. She's always wanted to publish a book, and set forth on the process by reaching out to many of her colleagues from UCR for guidance! *Besos* is original poetry written as well as edited by the Celeste.

Celeste is a storyteller and artist. The rawness and integrity in her words create powerful visuals and musicality to her work. Her goal of her art is that the audience finds a home and comfort in her work. She hopes to perform and tour her poetry to the world! Lastly, she hopes to create visual music videos for her poetry in the future.

ABOUT THE BOOK

Besos is meant to empower and inspire the audience. The book is planning to be translated in many languages as well as have an audiobook option! Thank you for coming to the end. This book took all of Celeste's soul to write, and she's super grateful for your support and love!

www.ingramcontent.com/pod-product-compliance
Lightning Source LLC
LaVergne TN
LVHW040736250326
834688LV00031B/327